Change is Coming: What is A Leader to Do?

By Dr. Angela R. Johnson

Edited by: Lewander G. Davis

Photography: Dawn Wilbert of QuicKnight Photography

ACKNOWLEDGMENT

I would like to acknowledge my parents, Joe and Clemmie Johnson for instilling in me Philippians 4:13 – I can do all things through Christ who strengthens me. I would like to thank my brother, Keith L. Johnson for encouraging me in my endeavors. I want to thank Lewander Davis for being available to assist in reviewing and editing my documents, as well as a great thought leader. Last, but surely not least, I thank God for pouring into me what he would have me to share to encourage His people.

All Scriptures denoted in this book are from the Holy Bible NIV or NLT.

DEDICATION

This book is dedicated to aspiring leaders and current leaders who are seeking to change their current condition. If you are not content in your current situation seek first the kingdom and His righteousness and all these things will be given to you as well (Matthew 6:33).

INTRODUCTION

If you are reading this, you have been involved in a change effort at work, church, home or school. Or, you may be tired of the status quo and are preparing to make changes within your organization or business. Change is inevitable. It happens every day. Some people handle change with ease and others are challenged with the thought of it. Never fear, change is manageable. Leaders are ultimately responsible for how people react and engage in change.

I had the opportunity to work for an organization where change is the norm. Regardless of the constant need for change, they are not welcomed. In the instance of this organization, change was required to save jobs. In response to the economic down turn of 2007/2008 in

Michigan, we had to look at how we performed work. Employees were tasked with removing waste from their job. Guess what? Nobody saw their job as being non-essential or any parts of it being wasteful. Hence, this was a challenge for the leadership team. The organization's leader was committed to not laying off workers, which would have contributed, to the existing dismal economic climate. The vision of the senior leader was to improve operational efficiency and provide the same or better level of service to the customers at the same cost. The plan the leader established was an excellent start in the change journey. Several continuous improvement initiatives were utilized to identify and implement cost saving measures for the organization. However, for continuous improvement efforts to be successful it was imperative for leadership to engage employees through obtaining input and buy-in from the people doing the work.

Leaders are to provide the vision and direction, but when it comes to implementing the vision, the workers performing the work must engage in the change journey. The journey of change has been lengthy and arduous for the organization I work for; I attribute that to the lack of understanding of how a leader's leadership style influences the engagement of the workers performing the work.

Whether we are ready or not, change is coming. What should a leader do? After years of observing and conducting research on leadership styles and employee engagement, three key measures were apparent for a leader to navigate change. First, the leader must have the courage to define the change and not deny it exists or is coming. Secondly, the leader must have influence and power to lead people through change. Lastly, the leader must have a vision to engage followers in the change.

COURAGEOUSLY DEFINE CHANGE

Change means to create something new or to modify an existing 'something', which provides improved functionality and performance. However, before something new is created, someone must express a need or recognize change is required (Brisson-Banks, 2010). The current state of the organization or entity in the midst of change or needing change should be fully understood before the change is defined. What does that mean? Before change is defined, the individuals impacted by it should understand why it is coming and needed. They need to see and understand the 'what's in it for me?' to be open and participate in the change. This means the leader has to communicate why change is required. Not only do they have to communicate it, the leader must ensure the employees fully understand why the change is required. In the event the leader's desired state or vision does not match an employee's viewpoint, it is possible for the employee not to engage in the organizational change.

I have had the opportunity to work for three fortune 500 companies, within three different industries. Each company has a distinct approach to engaging employees. My experience with the automotive industry demonstrated engagement through reward and punishment; whereas the appliance industry engagement of employees was lacking. Lastly, the utilities and energy industry has a culture of collaboration and buy-in.

Change specifically takes on many forms and is defined in various ways regardless of industry.

Organizational change is a change in product or service. It can also be defined in terms of a change in the leadership structure. Organizational change can also be categorized as strategic, structural, or job-related (Bordia, Hobman, Jones, Gallois, & Callan, 2004). Organizational change can be small or large (Beugelsdijk, Slangen, & Marco, 2002). The large or radical organizational changes are typically followed by the smaller, incremental changes that sustain the large changes made previously. Regardless of the category, context, type or definition of the change, the leader must have the courage to define it.

Leaders must be courageous in leading change, for the natural tendency of people is to resist and maintain the status quo. Joshua 1:8 begins "Be strong and courageous, for you are the one who will lead these people to possess all the land . . ." God commands us to be strong and courageous and not to be afraid or discouraged. Having the courage to direct change demonstrates strong leadership. Leaders must remember that God did not give us a spirit of fear and timidity (2 Timothy 1:7). Not only must a leader courageously define change, they should have influence and power to direct the change.

INFLUENCE AND LEADERSHIP STYLE

To implement and direct change, leaders should have the ability to influence the engagement of the employees or people performing the work to make the change happen. Hunter (1998) defines leadership as the ability to influence people to work passionately toward goals identified as being for the common good. Another author and motivational speaker, John Maxwell (1998) describes leadership as influence.

Different leadership styles influence followers differently. To gain a better understanding of how leadership styles influence engagement, specifically employees, I researched servant leadership, as well as conducted a study of 247 leaders on how transformational, transactional and laissez-faire leadership styles influenced a follower's engagement. The leaders were grouped into three different categories. Individuals who supervise employees and serve as a formal leader within an organization were categorized as bosses. Supervisors who are at the same level as employees they are providing work direction to were categorized as peers. Lastly, supervisors who are at a lower level than the employees they are providing work direction to be categorized as subordinates.

Transformational Leadership Style and Influence

My research results indicated a significant positive correlation in employee engagement with a transformational leadership style, by all three subgroups (bosses, peers and subordinates). There was a significant positive correlation in employee engagement with a supervisor who demonstrates a transformational leadership style. It was no surprise the transformational leadership style was positively correlated with employee engagement. The supervisor, who exhibits this leadership style, is focused on the needs of the employee. What employee would not want their leader to focus on their needs? The leader is also concerned with the relationship developed with the employee. Therefore, a leader with time to bond with employees would do well with the transformational leadership style, regardless of the supervisory hierarchy.

Servant Leadership and Influence

Servant leadership and transformational leadership have similarities. Hannay (2009) notes that both theories are people oriented leadership styles.

Although they are both people oriented, they relate to people differently. The servant leader is focused on *service* to the employee to facilitate a better employee. The transformational leader is focused on *engaging* the employee to support an organizational goal (Hannay, 2009). The common denominator is the employee. Transformational and servant leadership both work to engage and empower employees.

Hunter (1998) equates servant leadership with love as defined in 1 Corinthians chapter 13. It states that love is patient, kind, humble, respectful, honest, committed and forgiving. As a servant leader, a person should exhibit these qualities to fully engage the employee. Jesus is the ultimate servant leader. He built relationships with fishermen, zealots, tax collectors and

18

with other people who others thought unworthy (Youssef, 2013). Jesus looked for opportunities to encourage and mentor (Youssef, 2013). Hunter (1998) explains leadership is built on authority. He defines authority as the skill of getting the employee to willingly do the will of the leader because of the influence the leader has over the employee. Authority is built on service and sacrifice. Jesus made the ultimate sacrifice by dying on the cross for our sins so those who believe in him will have everlasting life. Service and sacrifice is built on love. "For God so loved the world that He gave His only begotten Son, that whosoever believes in Him should not perish but have everlasting life" (John 3:16). God's love is exhibited through Jesus' sacrifice. Love is built on will. Lastly, Hunter (1998) notes '*will*' is intentions in addition to actions. Servant leaders intentionally create the proper environment for their employees to grow. This act of love facilitates the relationship the leader needs to develop with the employee. The act of love from a leader to a follower can be exhibited through the fulfillment of the follower's *needs*. Servant leaders are about serving their subordinates.

Transactional Leadership Style and Influence

My research results also indicated a significant positive correlation in employee engagement with a supervisor demonstrating a transactional leadership style, regardless of their position level within the company. These results were opposite of my hypothesis, that there would be a negative correlation with a transactional leadership style and employee engagement. My research hypothesis was developed due to the belief that employees do not like to be told what to do. Unpredictably, the demographics of the research participants showed 39.3% of the survey respondents had five years or less of work experience. This suggests to a new supervisor more direction and oversight is required for employees with less work experience or unfamiliarity with the tasks being performed. Therefore a transactional leadership style will provide more influence on followers who are unfamiliar with what a leader wants done.

Laissez-Faire Leadership Style and Influence

Lastly, my research results indicated a significant negative association in employee engagement with

21

laissez-faire leadership style for employees who received work direction from a supervisor who was a superior, also known as 'the boss'. The laissez-faire leadership style is a hands off leadership approach. The hands off approach exhibited by a supervisor's unresponsiveness to an employee's problem and lack of monitoring work performance are not motivating to employees. However, the research results showed employees find it moderately acceptable for subordinates who provide work direction to have a hands off approach to supervising. Subordinates are not held to the same standards of supervision as superiors.

Regardless of a leader's leadership style, the key to influence and power is achieving a specific goal while the leader builds a relationship with the employees charged with performing the task. The leader's ability to

understand which leadership style to display in order to

draw out what they need from followers is essential in

driving change.

VISION

Leaders need to establish a vision their employees can come together around as a team (Covey, 2007). In addition to creating a vision, leaders should be able to communicate the vision and provide an environment for open and honest dialogue about the vision. The vision should depict a clear picture of what "good" looks like, so employees know when the vision is achieved. What does "good look like" is a term I have heard many times over the last few months.

As the leaders of the organization I work for communicate their vision, employees performing the work are asking, 'what does good look like?" My job has been to help define what 'good looks like'. Facilitating a vision to life requires understanding the leader and the employees. When a leader has a vision, that vision must be communicated such that the employee or follower knows what it looks like at their level.

Establishing and communicating a clear vision is essential for leaders specifically during changing times. A leader *should* challenge the status quo and use their influence, regardless of the leadership style exhibited, to achieve a goal (Brady & Woodward, 2012). Therefore, a leader is essential in changing the status quo. Brady and Woodward (2012) define influence as "Effort x Scope (or Reach)". A leader's effort times the amount of people they can reach equals their level of influence they have on change. What does this mean? This means the leader needs to invest in their team, their employees, and/or their followers. The investment or effort can be financial or emotional. It depends on the needs of the team, employees or followers. A leader needs to know the difference between needs and wants (Hunter, 1998). The effort or investment needs to be genuine and sincere. Great leaders do not mind being uncomfortable when changing to seek excellence, for they are frustrated with the status quo. Vision is about moving forward. What vision(s) do you have to birth?

WHAT IS A LEADER TO DO?

Leaders should exhibit the 2D's of change - *Drive and Desire*. Leaders must drive change by continually improving the performance of their organization. They should not be satisfied with the status quo and have the desire to improve the current condition. Regardless of where you are in the leadership chain, you have the potential to influence change. Leaders must establish a vision, set goals, devise a game plan, work the plan and seek counsel to check if the vision needs adjustment (Brady & Woodward, 2012). This is known as the cycle of achievement. Psalms 89: 19-20 describes how God chose and anointed David, a common man, to become king. Everyone is a leader in some regard. It is just a matter of time, when a person will need to show ***courage*** to step up and ***influence*** others with their power and wisdom to fulfill a ***vision***. Whether you are a leader of your home, at your school, place of employment or place of worship, change will come. What are *you* going to do?

REFERENCES

Beugelsdijk, S., Slangen, A., & Marco, v. H. (2002).
Shapes of organizational change: The case of
Heineken Inc. *Journal of Organizational Change
Management, 15*(3), 311-326.

Bordia, P., Hobman, E., Jones, E., Gallois, C., & Callan,
V. J. (2004). Uncertainty during organizational
change: Types, consequences, and management
strategies. *Journal of Business and Psychology,
18*(4), 507-532.

Brady, C. & Woodward, O. (2012). *Launching a
leadership revolution: Mastering the five levels of
influence.* Flint, MI: Obstacles Press.

Brisson-Banks, C. (2010). Managing change and
transitions: A comparison of different models and
their commonalities. *Library Management, 31*(4),
241-252.

Covey, S. R. (2007). *Leadership: The 4 imperatives of
great leaders.*New York, NY: Simon & Schuster.
Audiobook

Hannay, M. (2009, February). The cross-cultural leader: The application of servant leadership theory in the international context. *Journal of International Business and Cultural Studies,* 1-12.

Hunter, J. C. (1998). *The servant: A simple story about the true essence of leadership.* Roseville, CA: Prima Publishing.

Johnson, A. R. (2015). *The effect of leadership style on employee engagement within an organizational environment of change: A correlational study* (Order No. 3718636). Available from ProQuest Dissertations & Theses Full Text.

Maxwell, J.C. (1998). *The 21 irrefutable laws of leadership: follow them and people will follow you.* Nashville, TN: Thomas Nelson.

Youssef, M. (2013). *The leadership style of Jesus.* Oregon: Harvest House Publishers.

ABOUT THE AUTHOR

 ANGELA R JOHNSON has over 20 years experience in continuous improvement, quality management, and project management. Her professional background reflects achievements in leading process improvement initiatives, as well as teaching and mentoring individuals in Business Organization and Management; Critical Thinking; Lean Six Sigma and Quality Management principles. Angela has a Doctorate of Philosophy in Organization and Management, where her doctoral research focused on a leader's leadership style and employee engagement. She also holds a Master of Science degree in Administration and a Bachelor of Science degree in Engineering. Angela is an independent certified coach, teacher and speaker with The John Maxwell Team. Her passion is to transfer knowledge to facilitate operational excellence within organizations and people. She is also a part-time faculty member Schoolcraft College and University of Phoenix. Angela resides in southeast Michigan with her family.

www.ingramcontent.com/pod-product-compliance
Lightning Source LLC
Chambersburg PA
CBHW061235180526
45170CB00003B/1307